TEEN LIFE™

FREQUENTLY ASKED QUESTIONS ABOUT

Birth Control

Beverly Vincent
and Robert
Greenberger

WITHDRAWN

ROSEN
PUBLISHING®

New York

Published in 2012 by The Rosen Publishing Group, Inc.
29 East 21st Street, New York, NY 10010

Library of Congress Cataloging-in-Publication Data

Vincent, Beverly.
Frequently asked questions about birth control/Beverly Vincent, Robert Greenberger.—1st ed.
    p. cm.—(FAQ. teen life)
Includes bibliographical references and index.
ISBN 978-1-4488-5561-2 (library binding)
1. Contraception—Juvenile literature. 2. Birth control—Juvenile literature. I. Greenberger, Robert. II. Title.
RG136.3.V56 2012
618.18—dc23

2011013544

Manufactured in China

CPSIA Compliance Information: Batch #W12YA. For further information, contact Rosen Publishing, New York, New York, at 1-800-237-9932.

Contents

one

What Do You Need to Know About Birth Control?

One of the most challenging decisions many teenagers face today is whether to have sex. It is important for teens to think about their reasons for having sex. The following are some not-so-good reasons:

- Having sex maintains and improves the relationship.
- Sex makes you seem cool and more adult to others.
  - Curiosity.
  - "It just happened."
  - Desire to be popular and accepted.
- All your friends are "doing it."
- Someone dared you to do it or pressured you into it.

Whatever your reason is for having sex, it is your responsibility to have safer sex. Safer sex means protecting

If you and your partner decide to be sexually active, you first need to evaluate the ramifications of your decision and take proper steps for preventing pregnancy and STDs.

yourself from sexually transmitted diseases (STDs) and protecting yourself or your partner from pregnancy. Abstinence—not having oral, anal, or vaginal sex—is the only true form of safe sex. It is the only sure way to avoid pregnancy and prevent spreading STDs. If you choose to have sex, you must consider the consequences and take the appropriate and responsible measures to prevent pregnancy and STDs.

Whatever type of birth control—also called contraception— you choose, it should offer dual protection. First, it should protect against pregnancy. Second, and just as important, it should protect against getting potentially deadly sexually transmitted diseases such as the human immunodeficiency virus (HIV, which causes acquired immunodeficiency syndrome [AIDS]) as well as genital herpes and others. Effective contraception must serve these two critical purposes.

In recent years, there has been a decrease in teen pregnancies in the United States. However, teens in the United States still have more unintended pregnancies than teens in any other country. Of the nearly 750,000 teen pregnancies in the United States each year, 82 percent are unintended, according to the Guttmacher Institute (a nonprofit organization that works to educate the public about reproductive health research). In 2008, about 42 out of every 1,000 teenage girls became pregnant, as reported by the Centers for Disease Control and Prevention (CDC) in 2010. But more teenagers are now getting the facts and acting responsibly about sex.

Birth Control Methods

Choosing a birth control method is a big decision. Talking with your health-care provider is a good way to figure out which method is right for you. You can also talk to your partner, close friend, parent, or another trusted adult to see if he or she can help you make a decision. If you do not like one method, you can always try another. There are plenty of different options, so you should be able to find one that works for you.

You should know that birth control is available for people of all ages, without a parent's permission. It is illegal for your health-care provider to tell anyone if you ask for birth control. If you can talk to your parents about your decision to use birth control, that is great. However, if you can't, you should double-check with your health-care provider about what will be billed and if they will be contacting you by phone or mail.

Discussing birth control can be awkward and scary. It means not only talking about sex, but also talking about trust and honesty. If you are not able to talk about these things with your partner, perhaps you are not ready to be sexually active with him or her.

When it comes to safer sex, people need to be comfortable not only with each other, but also with themselves. They need to know the facts and feel comfortable talking about their bodies. In addition to being able to talk about their bodies, they should get to know their own bodies. In the end, it is up to you to act responsibly.

Many different kinds of birth control methods are available today. You should ask yourself four questions when deciding on the form of birth control that is best for you and your partner:

- How effective is it in preventing pregnancy and diseases?
- How safe is it to use?

There are a variety of brands and types of male condoms (which are also called rubbers or jimmies). Latex condoms can help to prevent the spread of some STDs and HIV (the virus that causes AIDS) better than those made of animal skin.

- Will it fit into my lifestyle?
- Can I afford it?

Some birth control methods are more effective and safer than others. If a contraceptive is not used in the right way, it will not work properly and you will run the risk of an unintended pregnancy.

Many young people think of birth control as a nuisance. Some feel it is not easy to use. Others believe it spoils the sexual mood. However, using birth control is smart and will prevent potentially serious problems in the future.

Use of each type of method requires advance planning. Some kinds of birth control can be put in place hours before sex, while others must be used right before having sex. Only the morning-after pill can be used after sex, and, partly due to its potentially serious side effects, it is for emergency use only, not routine contraception.

The minute or two it takes to use a contraceptive can make a big difference in protecting your health. A contraceptive can save your life and prevent an unplanned pregnancy.

Contraceptives on the Market

All legally sold contraceptives are safe to use, although some may have side effects if you use them for a long time. The use of some contraceptives is riskier for some people than for others.

Not every birth control method is right for every person. That is why you should speak with a doctor before you have sex. Your doctor can help you figure out which methods are best for you.

If you are female, your doctor can discuss the birth control pill with you and whether or not it's the right choice for you, given your needs, lifestyle, and particular health concerns. If you decide the Pill is for you, your doctor can prescribe it. Other products must also be prescribed and fitted by a doctor. For instance, a doctor helps fit women for diaphragms to make sure they will work properly.

If you have questions about the various options for contraception, talk to your doctor or a health-care professional at a family planning clinic.

two

How Do the Human Reproductive Systems Work?

The first step in knowing how to prevent pregnancy is to understand how the human body works. Men and women have different organs that make up their reproductive systems. It is through these organs acting together that men and women are able to create babies.

The Male Reproductive System

The male reproductive system produces sperm. Sperm, which are produced in the testicles, fertilize the female's eggs. The sperm travel from the testicles, through a tube called the vas deferens, to the prostate gland. The prostate gland produces a whitish liquid in which the sperm can swim easily. This liquid, combined with the sperm, is called semen. Semen exits the penis through the urethra.

When a man reaches orgasm and releases semen, it is called ejaculation. Before a man ejaculates, his penis releases a clear pre-ejaculatory fluid. This fluid cleans the path for the sperm and provides lubrication. Pre-ejaculatory fluid does not contain sperm but may carry STDs, including HIV, which causes AIDS. To avoid STDs, men should make sure that no pre-ejaculatory fluid gets inside their partners.

Sperm live best in a temperature lower than 98.6 degrees Fahrenheit (37 degrees Celsius), the body's normal temperature. The testicles are in a sac outside the body, called the scrotum, which keeps the sperm cooler than the internal body temperature.

When the male is excited, his penis rises and becomes hard. This is called an erection. When he is completely stimulated, the male has an orgasm, which leads to ejaculation. The average ejaculation contains up to 500 million sperm and would fill about

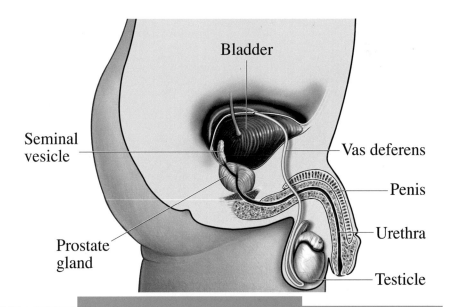

The male reproductive system is made up of the testicles, the duct system, glands (including seminal vesicles and prostate), and the penis. The male reproductive organs are located inside and outside the pelvis.

half a teaspoon. Only one of those 500 million sperm is needed to impregnate a woman.

The Female Reproductive System

Unlike male genitals, the female reproductive system consists mainly of organs not visible on the outside of the body. The visible parts are the labia and the pubic hair that covers them. The labia start at the clitoris, which is a bump about the size of a small pea, under the pubic bone. During sex, the clitoris, which is filled with many sensitive nerve endings, becomes stimulated and enlarged. When the clitoris becomes fully aroused, a woman has an orgasm. During orgasm, a woman's vaginal muscles contract, and she may release some liquid from the vaginal opening. This liquid is called vaginal fluid.

Some women are born with a thin membrane that partially covers the opening of the vagina, called the hymen. The first few times a woman has intercourse, her unstretched hymen can cause pain. There may also be some bleeding. Once the hymen is stretched, however, sex is not uncomfortable.

The walls of the vagina are soft folds of skin that lead to the cervix, the opening to the uterus, or womb. Sperm travel through the cervix to reach the uterus. On either side of the uterus are the fallopian tubes. At the end of the fallopian tubes are the ovaries, where the eggs are stored. Every month, one egg is released from an ovary. This is called ovulation. The egg travels to the uterus through a fallopian tube. If one sperm enters the fallopian tube while an egg is there, it can fertilize the

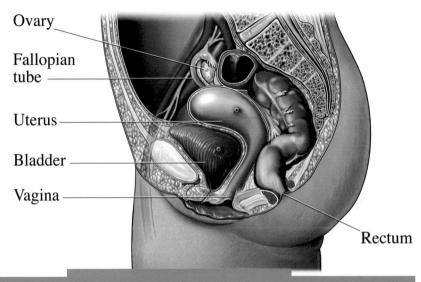

Ovary

Fallopian tube

Uterus

Bladder

Vagina

Rectum

The female reproductive system includes the vagina, uterus, fallopian tubes, and ovaries. The vagina, the canal that joins the cervix (the lower portion of the uterus) to the outside of a woman's body, is also called the birth canal.

egg. The fertilized egg would then travel down to the uterus and implant itself. This is how the woman becomes pregnant.

Menstruation and Fertility

Women's fertility is regulated by a cycle called the menstrual cycle, or "period," which most women start experiencing between the ages of nine and fifteen. The menstrual cycle usually takes about twenty-eight days to be completed. The middle of the cycle is when a woman is the most fertile. Ovulation—the time when an egg is released into a fallopian tube—occurs during that time in the middle of the cycle. Therefore, a woman's fertility is at its peak during ovulation.

This cycle means that each month the female body has a chance of becoming pregnant. The walls of the uterus become thick with tissue that can feed a fertilized egg. If the woman's egg is not fertilized and implanted that month, the thickened

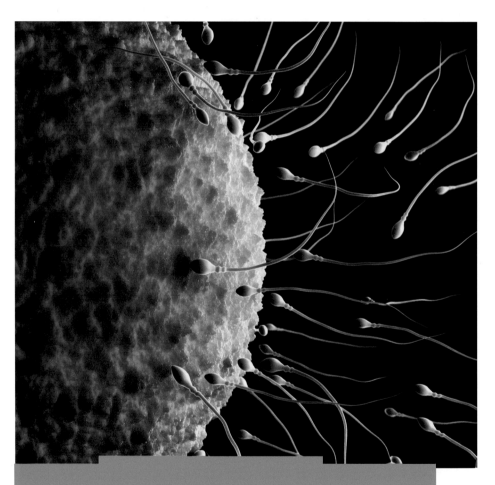

Sperm enter an ovum, or egg. Conception, the fertilization of a woman's egg by a man's sperm, usually occurs in the fallopian tubes.

lining of the uterus is shed. The lining falls off the wall of the uterus and travels down through the cervix. From the cervix, it flows out of the vagina. This marks the "period" stage of the cycle, when the woman experiences bleeding.

The average time between a woman's periods is about twenty-eight days. The amount of bleeding each woman experiences is different. On average, a woman bleeds from three to seven days. The heaviest bleeding is usually in the first two days.

Fertility is related to the menstrual cycle. The menstrual cycle begins with the onset of a woman's period (the time in which she is bleeding). During the second week of the cycle (after bleeding stops), the ovaries produce more of the female hormone estrogen. The estrogen stimulates about six eggs in the ovaries. Only one egg will grow large enough to survive. The others will stop growing and dissolve into the body.

By the end of the second week, the egg is ready. Before it is released, a pool of fluid grows around it. The fluid is called a follicle. The follicle then breaks open and releases the egg. The egg is released into the fallopian tube (ovulation), where it can be fertilized.

Once the egg is released, it must be fertilized within twenty-four hours. Sperm can live three to seven days inside the female body. A woman can become pregnant if she has unprotected sex three to seven days before she ovulates because the sperm could still be present when the egg is released. If the egg is not fertilized, it travels down the fallopian tube to the uterus.

The days right before and during ovulation are a woman's most fertile days. But that does not mean a woman cannot get pregnant during the other days of the month. In fact, a woman can become pregnant at any time during the month. Changes in the ovulation cycle can occur every month, which can make fertile days hard to predict. Women may have sex thinking that they are safe, but they are putting themselves at risk of becoming pregnant. Unprotected sex is very risky at any time of the month.

The Teenage Body

Adolescence and puberty are times of great change. They are the transition stages from childhood to adulthood, characterized by emotional and physical change. Puberty usually occurs between the ages of nine and fourteen.

Many of the body's changes during puberty involve the sexual and reproductive organs. Most changes are caused by an increase in hormones.

In addition to physical changes, teens must also deal with emotional changes. With the growth of the genitals and the increase in hormones, teens begin to think about sex.

Puberty and Fertility in Young Men

Usually the first external sign of puberty in young men is pubic hair growth. Then the testicles and penis grow larger. Often, this is also the time when a boy's voice changes and gets deeper. Armpit hair and facial hair begin to grow. Some boys experience a growth spurt and get taller very quickly. Many boys also develop acne or pimples. A young man in puberty will probably have what are called wet dreams. He dreams about sex, has an orgasm, and his body releases semen. This is entirely normal and common.

Puberty and Fertility in Young Women

The first sign of puberty in girls is the growth of breasts, called breast budding. The next sign is pubic hair, and then hair growing in the armpits.

The last sign of puberty is when a girl gets her period. Girls usually get their first periods at around the age of twelve, but getting a period anytime between the ages of nine and eighteen is normal. Although somewhat unusual, it is possible for a girl to get pregnant before getting her first period.

A doctor who provides medical care for women's reproductive organs is known as a gynecologist. Young women should see a gynecologist once every year if they are thinking about becoming sexually active, if they are sexually active, or once they turn eighteen. The gynecologist can answer any questions a young woman may have about her changing body. He or she can also give advice about the best type of birth control for each individual.

three

How Effective Are Abstinence, Periodic Abstinence, and Withdrawal?

Every person has a different pattern of sexual behavior. Some people choose to have sex often. Others choose to have sex only once in a while. Some choose not to have sex at all. The number of times you have sex will help you decide which birth control method is best for you.

Abstinence

Abstinence means not having vaginal, oral, or anal sex. Abstinence is the only way to make sure that neither partner contracts STDs and that the woman does not get pregnant. A couple practicing abstinence can kiss, rub against each other with their clothes on, and touch each other's genitals with their fingers. But one person's sexual fluid (semen, pre-ejaculatory fluid, or vaginal

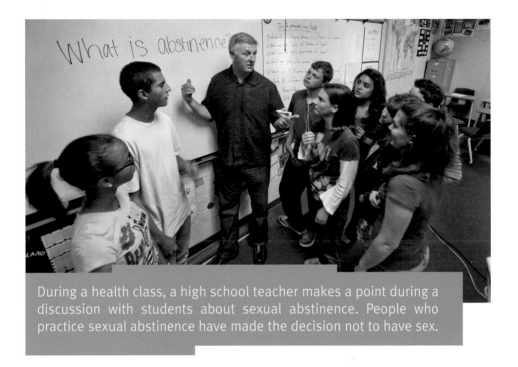

What is abstinence?

During a health class, a high school teacher makes a point during a discussion with students about sexual abstinence. People who practice sexual abstinence have made the decision not to have sex.

fluid) should not come into contact with the partner's mouth, anus, or genitals.

Many people think that the penis must enter the vagina for a woman to get pregnant, but that is not always true. Pregnancy can occur whenever a penis releases sperm in or near the vagina. If semen gets on the woman's thigh, the sperm could enter the vagina. If sperm get on the fingers of the man or the woman, and those fingers touch or enter the vagina, there is a possibility that a woman can get pregnant. The chances of pregnancy in these situations are very low, but they do exist.

There is no risk of pregnancy or STDs from masturbation, or self-stimulation. Masturbation is a healthy and safe way to explore your own body.

Periodic Abstinence

Periodic abstinence, also known as the rhythm method or natural family planning, is abstaining from sex during a woman's most fertile time. This can be complicated because a woman's ovulation is often irregular and difficult to track. A woman is fertile for longer than just the day she ovulates. An egg will stay fertile in a woman's fallopian tube for twenty-four hours after ovulation. Sperm can live in the vagina for three to five days. To be safe, a woman must avoid having sex for the five days before she ovulates, the day of ovulation, and the three days afterward.

For adults, periodic abstinence is effective approximately 75 percent of the time, according to an article by Omnia M. Samra-Latif on emedicine.medscape.com. This means that twenty-five out of one hundred women who practice periodic abstinence get pregnant. This is not a recommended method of birth control. In

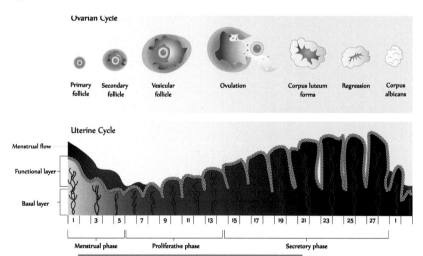

The top of this chart depicts the ovarian cycle and changes in a follicle's development. The bottom shows the uterine cycle and changes in hormone levels and the lining of the uterus during a typical monthly menstrual cycle. People who use periodic abstinence track ovulation to prevent pregnancy.

addition, this method does not protect either person from contracting an STD.

Withdrawal

Withdrawal is not recommended, especially for teenagers. To practice withdrawal, a man removes his penis from a woman's vagina before he ejaculates. Unfortunately, withdrawal is effective only 73 percent of the time, as reported by Planned Parenthood. Twenty-seven out of one hundred women who use this method become pregnant.

The following are a few reasons why this method of birth control does not work very well:

- It is often difficult for a man to pull his penis out of a woman's vagina when he is very excited.
- Many men cannot tell when they are about to have an orgasm and, therefore, do not pull out in time. For younger men and those with less sexual experience, ejaculation can happen a lot faster than they think it will.
- If a man has ejaculated recently, there may be sperm on the head of his penis. In addition, pre-ejaculatory fluid may push lingering sperm from an earlier ejaculation out of the urethra. To prevent this from occurring, always urinate after an ejaculation and before having sex again. This can also help prevent infections.

Withdrawal is a very risky birth control method. The woman could become pregnant, and neither partner is protected from STDs.

Myths and Facts

Birth control is my partner's responsibility.

Fact: → Women and men should share the responsibility of both buying and using birth control.

If I wash out my vagina after sex, I won't get pregnant.

Fact: → Given the speed of the sperm, there's no guarantee that washing with soap or a douche will stop the sperm from fertilizing an egg. Any additional liquid in the vagina, like douche, may actually help push the sperm farther inside and reach the egg.

The morning-after pill is a pill for abortion.

Fact: → Abortion terminates a pregnancy. Emergency contraception, or the morning-after pill, prevents the release of the egg or fertilization of the egg.

four

What Do You Need to Know About the Pill, Diaphragm, and Cervical Cap?

Hormonal birth control is commonly known as the Pill. It is very reliable and easy to use. The only important thing to remember is that it must be taken once every day at the same time of the day.

How Does the Pill Work?

Most types of birth control pills are combination pills containing two hormones, estrogen and progestin (a synthetic type of the naturally occurring hormone progesterone). They are human-made versions of the hormones a woman's body normally produces. The hormones trick the body into thinking it is pregnant. As a result, the ovaries do not release new eggs in the middle of each monthly cycle.

Without the release of eggs, there is practically no chance of pregnancy.

There's another birth control pill that is a progestin-only pill. This pill is sometimes known as the mini-pill. Because it contains only one kind of hormone, progestin, it works by changing the cervical mucus (by making it thicker) and the uterus lining (by making it thinner). It can also affect ovulation. However, it might be somewhat less effective in preventing pregnancy that the combination pill. To work as intended, the mini-pill must be taken every day at the same time of the day.

Taking the Pill

The Pill is taken orally every day. Most prescriptions offer pills in packages that will last for a whole month (twenty-eight pills). Pills taken in the first three weeks contain the hormone combination, while the final week's pills are inactive. They contain no hormones and simply keep you in the habit of taking your daily pill. Other versions will offer a three-week supply of the Pill (twenty-one pills) with instructions not to take a pill for the remaining seven days in the cycle. Follow the instructions on the package to make sure you take the correct pill on the correct day. It is necessary to take the Pill at the same time every day.

Another type of combination pill prescription has been developed recently that contains twelve weeks' worth of combination pills, followed by a week's worth of nonactive pills (containing no hormones). This low-dose pill decreases the frequency of a woman's period, from monthly to once every three months. This

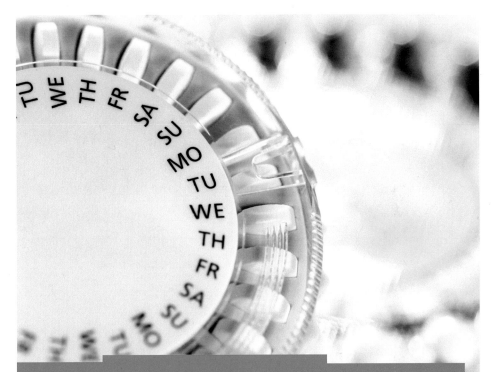

Most birth control pills are packaged as twenty-one or twenty-eight-day units and many are stored in a plastic tablet dispenser case, labeled with the days of the week. Some fashionable brands also have an alarm that reminds you to take your pill at the same time every day.

type of low-dose pill has been determined to be a less effective form of birth control than the traditional Pill.

What If You Forgot to Take the Pill?

The Pill does not work if it is not taken according to schedule. If a woman forgets to take one, her chances of pregnancy become greater for the rest of that month. There are some ways to reduce the risks if a pill is missed. If one pill is missed, take two pills the next day as soon as you remember. Then go back to the normal schedule. If two pills are missed, you need to take two pills for the next two days. Then go back to the normal schedule. This method only helps reduce the chances of pregnancy; it is not absolutely effective. If you miss a pill, you should always call your doctor and ask for his or her advice on how to proceed. After missing a pill, it is a good idea to use an additional method of birth control whenever you have sex until the next cycle—and the next package of pills—begins. It is always a good idea to call your health-care provider if you have any questions or concerns.

To Stop Taking the Pill

Stopping the Pill is easy. You just stop taking it. Your periods may be irregular for a while, but other than that, you should notice no problems. Just remember that as soon as you stop taking the Pill, you could get pregnant. You need to use some other form of contraception.

The Pill's Side Effects

There are usually some side effects with the Pill, which vary from person to person. These include increased breast size or breast tenderness, bloating, weight gain, nausea, vomiting, and depression. Many of these symptoms usually go away by the third month. To avoid nausea, women can take the Pill on a full stomach or just before bed. If a woman is unhappy with the side effects, her doctor can prescribe a different brand of pill after the third month. Different brands have different effects on different people.

Some women also experience irregular bleeding with the Pill. They may menstruate mid-cycle, or their period may not come at all. Women who miss a period after taking the Pill should notify their doctor.

Advantages and Disadvantages of the Pill

Most women should feel safe taking the Pill. In addition to being an effective form of contraception, the Pill has many health benefits. It can decrease acne and protect against certain kinds of cancer and ovarian cysts. Many women report that it results in lighter periods with milder cramps. However, women who are at risk for certain diseases, such as high blood pressure, diabetes, high cholesterol, blood-clotting disorders, or heart disease, increase their risk if they use the Pill. Moreover, many doctors will not prescribe the Pill for women who smoke cigarettes because that combination increases the harmful effects of cigarettes.

Obtaining the Pill

The Pill cannot be bought over the counter. You must have a prescription from a doctor, most often from a gynecologist. Once on the Pill, women are recommended to have regular examinations. If sexually active, checkups are recommended every six to twelve months.

Emergency Contraception

You may have heard of emergency contraception, also called the morning-after pill, a very controversial form of contraception. It is also known as Plan B and Next Choice, after brand names of this type of pill. The morning-after pill, which contains a high concentration of levonorgestrel, can prevent a pregnancy if it is taken seventy-two hours after unprotected sex. Here are the advantages of the morning-after pill:

- It prevents the woman's egg from being released.
- It makes sperm's travel more difficult.
- The pill helps prevent a fertilized egg from implanting into the uterus.

The following are the possible side effects of taking the morning-after pill:

- Nausea
- Vomiting
- Breast tenderness
- Ectopic pregnancy (which can be life-threatening)
- Blood-clot formation

In 2006, the U.S. Food and Drug Administration (FDA), after carefully studying the short- and long-term effects of the medication, approved the drug for sale to the general public. In 2009, the FDA reached agreement with the drug's manufacturer to make the drug available over the counter to anyone age seventeen or older and by prescription to anyone under age seventeen.

Taking this pill does not cause an abortion because it does not end an existing pregnancy. Instead, it prevents a pregnancy from occurring. Eighty-two percent of women who use the morning-after pill do not get pregnant. It is recommended for women whose regular method of birth control fails, like when a condom breaks. The morning-after pill is not for everyday use. In fact, health experts refer to it solely as emergency contraception.

If you obtain Plan B, the pack will contain two pills. The instructions on the Plan B pack may direct you to take the first pill as soon as possible, followed by the second pill twelve hours later. However, research has shown that the Plan B pills are just as effective regardless of whether the two pills are taken at the same time or taken twelve hours apart.

The Diaphragm

A diaphragm is a latex or silicone cup that is filled with spermicide and inserted into the vagina. In the vagina, it rests against the pubic bone and covers the opening to the cervix. The diaphragm will block most of the sperm from entering the uterus. The spermicide will kill any sperm that may have passed around the diaphragm.

Diaphragms come in many different sizes. That is because women have different-sized pubic bones and cervixes. Each woman must be fitted for a diaphragm. A doctor will give you the appropriate-sized diaphragm for your body and will show you how to put it in and take it out. After a little practice, anyone can get the hang of it and insert the diaphragm quickly and correctly.

How to Use a Diaphragm

A diaphragm can be put in up to six hours before sex. Fill the diaphragm about two-thirds full of spermicidal jelly and smear a

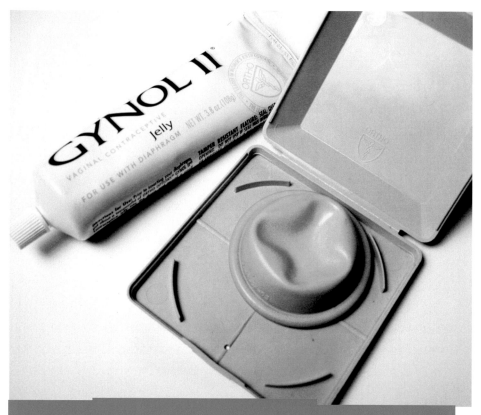

Spermicidal jelly should be properly applied to a diaphragm before inserting it. After using a diaphragm, it should be washed with mild soap and warm water, air dried, and then stored in a protective case. A diaphragm should be checked regularly for holes and to make sure it still fits correctly.

bit around the edges. This makes it easier to insert and provides additional spermicidal protection. Then the diaphragm is pinched together with one hand. The other hand separates the lips of the vagina. The diaphragm is then inserted into the vagina as far as it will go. It should rest over the cervix and against the pubic bone. It is easiest to do this in one of three positions: 1) lying on your back, knees up; 2) squatting; or 3) standing, with one leg propped up on the sink or toilet seat.

It is easy to check the position of the diaphragm by inserting a finger into the vagina. The edge of the diaphragm should be up against the pubic bone. Once a diaphragm is in, it is very hard for it to rest in any position that is not the right one. The diaphragm must stay in for six to eight hours after sex but it should not be worn for more than twenty-four hours at one time. You'll need to add more spermicide before additional acts of sex. Most women can walk around with the diaphragm inside of them without any discomfort. If you are unsure if it is in correctly, you can insert it and have your health-care provider double-check.

The diaphragm can be removed easily by placing your fingers into your vagina, then reaching up and hooking the rim with your finger. The diaphragm will slide out.

Caring for Your Diaphragm

Once you remove the diaphragm, wash it with a mild soap (one that does not contain perfume) and water. Be sure to rinse it thoroughly. Dry the diaphragm completely and store it in its carrying case in a cool, dry place. A diaphragm can dry out and crack if it is left out in the air for too long.

It is important to wash and dry your diaphragm after each use and again before the next use. The only substances that should go on it are spermicidal jellies (sperm-killing substances). Be sure that the jelly you use is made for use with diaphragms. The jellies that are not meant for use with diaphragms can cause the rubber to crack.

Always remember to check your diaphragm for holes or tears. This can be done by holding it up to the light or by filling it with water to see if it leaks. If there are any holes or cracks, throw it out and get a new one. You need to have your diaphragm replaced at least every two years. You should also be refitted for a diaphragm if you have gained or lost more than ten pounds (4.5 kilograms).

Advantages of Using a Diaphragm

There are several benefits to using a diaphragm, including the following:

- Diaphragms have almost no health risks or side effects. There are latex-free diaphragms, which are made of silicone. The spermicides used with diaphragms may even reduce the spread of certain STDs.
- It can be inserted up to six hours before intercourse, so you don't need to stop everything just before intercourse to get your contraception in place.
- The diaphragm contains no hormones.
- A diaphragm stops the flow of menstrual blood if you have sex during menstruation.

Disadvantages of Using a Diaphragm

The following are some drawbacks to using a diaphragm:

- Some people may be allergic or sensitive to the latex that most diaphragms are made of or to the spermicide used with a diaphragm.

WHAT DO YOU NEED TO KNOW ABOUT THE PILL,
DIAPHRAGM, AND CERVICAL CAP?

33

- A diaphragm alone doesn't protect against STDs. For maximum protection against both pregnancy and STDs, combine the use of a diaphragm with spermicide and a male condom.
- You must have a prescription to get a diaphragm.
- Some people don't feel comfortable inserting or taking out the diaphragm.

The Cervical Cap

The cervical cap, also called the FemCap, is a smaller version of the diaphragm. It is a small rubberlike cap made of silicone that is fitted snugly over the cervix and can be worn for up to

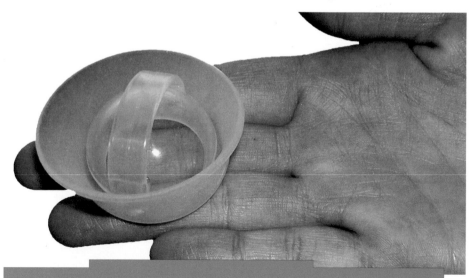

A cervical cap is a reusable contraceptive device that is used with a spermicide and is inserted into a woman's vagina. The FemCap, the cervical cap that is available in the United States, forms a tight seal around the cervix to block sperm from entering the uterus.

forty-eight hours. Unlike the diaphragm, it is not necessary to reapply spermicide for repeated intercourse.

According to the FDA, 17 to 23 percent of the women who rely on the cervical cap might become pregnant within a year. For best protection against pregnancy and STDs, the cervical cap should be used with a male condom. The cap must be left in place for six hours after intercourse. Care and maintenance of the cervical cap are the same as that for the diaphragm.

Check with your gynecologist or local clinic to find out whether the cap is available in your area.

WHAT DO YOU NEED TO KNOW ABOUT THE PILL, DIAPHRAGM, AND CERVICAL CAP?

35

Ten Great Questions to Ask Your Doctor

1 Is the birth control pill safe?

2 What is the best method of contraception for me?

3 What happens if I stop taking the Pill but I don't get a period?

4 Will the Pill protect me from STDs, including HIV?

5 Does using the Patch (Ortho Evra) have any side effects?

6 How long can I use the birth control shot?

7 How does an IUD work and how long will it last?

8 Do my girlfriend and I have to use a spermicide with a male condom?

9 Do I have to use a new female condom every time I have sex?

10 How often do I have to be checked by my gynecologist to make sure that my diaphragm still fits me properly?

five

How Safe Are Male Condoms and Spermicides?

A male condom is a rubberlike barrier that should be fitted over the erect penis before sex. A condom prevents sperm from coming into contact with your partner. Condoms are also known as rubbers and prophylactics. They are a very effective method of contraception. Health clinics and campus health centers often give out free condoms.

Condoms are different from other birth control methods primarily because they are the only common form of birth control used by the man. Condoms are also the only form of birth control that provides protection against sexually transmitted diseases because they form an impermeable shield between partners' genitals and prevent the exchange of body fluids between them. Condoms also lessen the amount of skin-to-skin contact between partners.

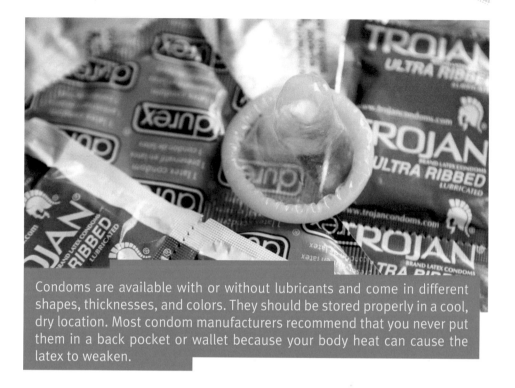

Condoms are available with or without lubricants and come in different shapes, thicknesses, and colors. They should be stored properly in a cool, dry location. Most condom manufacturers recommend that you never put them in a back pocket or wallet because your body heat can cause the latex to weaken.

Using a Condom

Condoms can be bought in many stores, including drugstores and supermarkets. In some states, school nurses or health teachers are required to hand out condoms upon request. Condoms come in different sizes, but latex stretches enough to fit most men.

The condom needs to be put on when the man's penis is erect. Although there may or may not be sperm in his pre-ejaculatory fluid, the fluid may contain an STD virus or bacteria. Therefore, it is a good idea to put the condom on before any of the fluid begins to appear at the tip of the penis.

When putting the condom on, it is important that it is right side up. There are two ways to tell if it is. First, an unrolled condom looks like the brim of a hat when it is right side up and like the dome of a temple when it is upside down. Second, if the condom does not unroll easily, it is upside down. If you try to put the condom on upside down and it touches the penis, do not turn it over and use that condom. Throw it away—it could have come into contact with pre-ejaculatory fluid.

Some men like to put a few drops of lubricant on the tip of the penis before putting on the condom. This increases sensation. Only water-based lubricants, such as KY Jelly or AstroGlide, should be used with latex. Never use oil-based products, like Vaseline or cooking oil, as lubricants; the oil can cause the latex to disintegrate and break. Water-based lubricants are widely available and are usually displayed next to the condoms.

When putting on the condom, pinch the tip to leave an airless area, or vacuum, that will hold the sperm when ejaculating. If the man is not circumcised, he should pull back his foreskin before unrolling the condom. Then he should unroll the condom down the base of the penis, making sure to smooth out any air bubbles but keeping the air space at the tip of the penis. Having intercourse with a condom full of air bubbles can cause the condom to break.

The man should withdraw his penis from his partner right after he ejaculates. The penis often gets soft soon after an orgasm. When the penis gets soft, the condom can slip off easily and sperm could then leak into his partner. When withdrawing from his partner, the man should hold the condom at the base of his penis. He should take the condom off away from his partner, in case any semen spills. Condoms should be wrapped in tissues or toilet paper and thrown away in a garbage can, not flushed down the toilet (they can clog a toilet and are not biodegradable).

Traditionally, condoms have been made from latex. But you may have seen newer polyurethane condoms, too. Some people claim that polyurethane condoms are more sensitive than latex ones because they are thinner in texture. But studies show that polyurethane condoms are not as effective in protecting against pregnancy and sexually transmitted diseases. Polyurethane condoms are more likely to slip off the penis during withdrawal and also to break. The bottom line is, unless you are among the small number of people allergic to latex, latex condoms are a far safer option.

Helpful Tips

You must use a fresh condom each time you have sex. Some condoms are coated with spermicide. This spermicide makes these condoms an even more effective method of birth control. When used consistently and correctly, condoms can be 98 percent effective. That effectiveness improves further if the condom contains spermicide or the woman uses spermicide. Condoms are usually available in packages of three or a dozen.

Spermicides and Nonoxynol-9

Spermicides are chemicals that kill sperm. They come as vaginal suppositories, film, foam, gels, and creams. They are available without a prescription and are fairly cheap and easy to use. Twenty-six women out of one hundred who used spermicides alone became pregnant in the course of one year, according to a report in 2010 by the National Institutes of Health. The rather high pregnancy rate is the reason why this method is often used in combination with another method of birth control.

Spermicides should be used with condoms for maximum protection against pregnancy. A new application of spermicide should be used before each act of sex. It provides protection for about one hour.

Nonoxynol-9 kills sperm and is the active ingredient in most over-the-counter spermicides. But nonoxynol-9 does NOT protect you from contracting the HIV virus (which causes AIDS) or other sexually transmitted diseases such as gonorrhea or chlamydia. Moreover, although nonoxynol-9 can be used alone in cream or gel form, it is also used as a spermicide within condoms. But

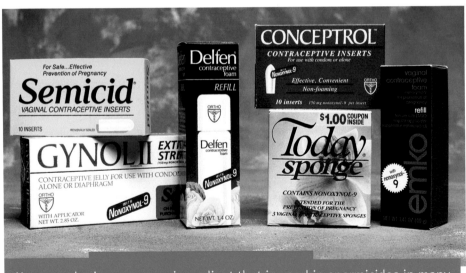

Nonoxynol-9 is a common ingredient that is used in spermicides in many birth control products. According to the FDA, medical studies have shown that the nonoxynol-9 spermicides do not prevent or reduce the risk of getting HIV. These spermicides can cause vaginal irritation that could actually increase the risk of getting HIV from an infected partner.

there is also no evidence that condoms lubricated with nonoxynol-9 are any more effective in preventing pregnancy or infection than condoms lubricated with silicone, according to the World Health Organization (WHO). Last, frequent use of vaginal contraceptives with nonoxynol-9 can also cause vaginal irritation and lesions (small cuts) in the vaginal wall, which can actually increase the likelihood of HIV infection. For all these reasons, many members of the medical community advise against the use of nonoxynol-9 as a means of birth control. Alternative spermicides containing oxtoxynol-9 can be used instead.

Suppositories, Films, Jellies, Creams, and Foams

Vaginal suppositories are inserted into the vagina. Vaginal films are paper-thin, 2-inch (5.08-centimeter) square sheets of film containing spermicide. Both suppositories and films must be inserted far into the vagina, on or near the cervix. Depending on the brand, they take ten to fifteen minutes to dissolve in the vagina before they are effective.

Spermicidal jellies and creams are usually applied to the inside of a diaphragm or cervical cap. If used alone, they are placed in the vagina with a special applicator, which is usually included in the package. The applicator is filled with the jelly or cream, and then gently inserted into the vagina. Each time you have sex, you must use a new dose of cream or jelly.

Spermicidal foams are also inserted into the vagina with an applicator. Foams usually come in containers that must be shaken well before use. Foam gives protection right after it is applied and lasts for an hour.

Advantages and Disadvantages of Spermicides

There are some major benefits of using spermicides. Besides being a contraceptive, spermicides also lubricate the vagina. Lubrication often makes sex more comfortable and enjoyable. Spermicides may also protect against spreading certain STDs, though the research on this effect remains inconclusive.

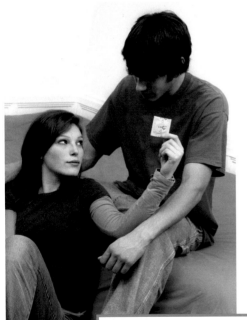

As for some of their drawbacks, spermicides can be inconvenient to use because they cannot be inserted more than fifteen minutes before sex. They can also be messy. Spermicides are not as effective by themselves as they are when coupled with other forms of birth control, such as a diaphragm or condom.

Spermicidal condoms contain a lubricant made of chemicals that help to decrease the number of living sperm. Although there is no 100 percent guarantee that people will not get STDs while using a condom, most medical experts believe that people can greatly reduce their chances of getting some STDs by using condoms properly.

Condoms with Spermicides

Many people choose to use condoms with spermicides. That means that the man wears a condom and the woman inserts spermicide into her vagina. Or the couple can use a condom that already contains spermicides. This method is an excellent one for a few reasons. First, both spermicides and condoms are available over the counter, which means that you can get them without a prescription. Second, this method is as effective as the birth control pill. It is the best-known way, other than abstinence, to prevent against some STDs. Third, both partners can participate in preventing pregnancy and protecting themselves from getting some STDs.

What Are Some Other Methods of Birth Control?

The past few years have brought new birth control methods, broadening the options available to you and your partner. Like the older methods, each new type of birth control has its advantages and disadvantages.

The Birth Control Shot

Depo-Provera—sometimes simply called the Shot—is an injection of the hormone progestin that prevents pregnancy for three months. A health-care professional gives a shot in your buttocks or upper arm. The hormone stops ovulation and makes sperm travel and egg implantation more difficult. Depo-Provera is highly effective about 97 percent of the time, according to the Mayo Clinic.

Depo-Provera has side effects similar to the Pill. It can cause weight gain, increased breast size, headaches, or depression. A woman using Depo-Provera may have

44

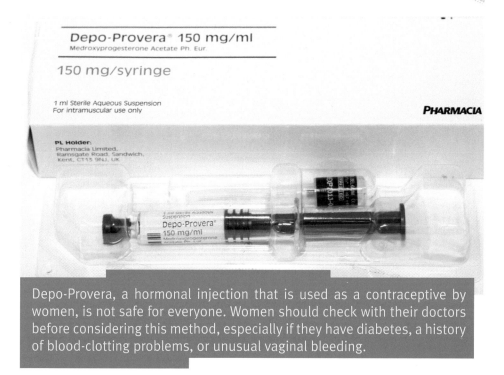

Depo-Provera 150 mg/ml
Medroxyprogesterone Acetate Ph. Eur.

150 mg/syringe

1 ml Sterile Aqueous Suspension
For intramuscular use only

PHARMACIA

PL Holder:
Pharmacia Limited,
Ramsgate Road, Sandwich,
Kent, CT13 9NJ, UK

Depo-Provera, a hormonal injection that is used as a contraceptive by women, is not safe for everyone. Women should check with their doctors before considering this method, especially if they have diabetes, a history of blood-clotting problems, or unusual vaginal bleeding.

spotting or missed periods. It may also take her up to a year to get pregnant after going off Depo-Provera, but it may not take any time at all. It does not protect against STDs. Doctors have still not determined if using Depo-Provera has long-term side effects, although they recommend not to use this method for more than two consecutive years because it may cause loss of bone density. People who choose Depo-Provera as their birth control method are advised to take calcium supplements. Many people choose Depo-Provera because it is long-lasting, doesn't require daily ingestion, and does not interrupt sexual intercourse.

The Female Condom

The female condom resembles the male condom, except that it is larger and has a ring on the inside. The woman squeezes the inner ring and inserts it into her vagina until it hits the cervix. The outer rim covers the labia and the penis during sexual intercourse. Depending on how well it is used, the female condom is between 79 and 95 percent effective at preventing pregnancy, according to the CDC. The Female Health Company, based in Chicago, Illinois, makes the FC2 female condom, and it was approved by the FDA for sale in the United States in 2009. It is sold under several brand names, including Reality.

The female condom is made of synthetic nitrile, which is good news for people with latex allergies. This material allows for affordability and comfort. Unlike the male condom, the female condom can be inserted up to twenty-four hours prior to sexual activity. Just like the male condom, the female condom may help to protect against the spread of STDs and HIV.

The Intrauterine Device

The intrauterine device, or IUD, is a T-shaped device that a doctor inserts into the uterus. It makes sperm travel more difficult, makes the sperm less likely to fertilize an egg, and prevents fertilized eggs from implanting in the uterus. The IUD is 99.4 percent effective.

Currently, there are two types available: ParaGard and Mirena. ParaGard uses a small copper wire wrapped around the IUD's plastic body and should not be used by anyone who is allergic to copper. The ParaGard IUD works up to twelve years. Mirena, approved by the FDA in 2000, releases small amounts of the synthetic hormone progestin. The hormone was added to attempt to decrease the bleeding and cramping that some women have with the IUD. The Mirena IUD works up to five years.

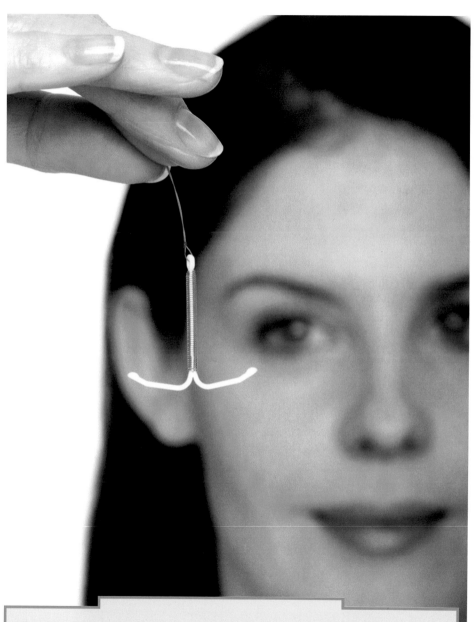

The hormonal and copper IUDs are T-shaped. The hormonal IUD, Mirena, releases a form of progestin and is effective for about five years once a doctor implants it in the uterus. The copper IUD, ParaGard, can stay in place for up to twelve years after it has been implanted.

Many doctors prefer to prescribe IUDs only to women who have had at least one child. This is because IUDs, which do not protect against STDs, can make some STDs more likely to cause infertility if not treated. People who have not had children tend to reject the IUD because it doesn't sit as well in the uterus. Other health concerns include longer, heavier, and more painful menstrual periods, which in turn might cause anemia. Some forms of the IUD can cause weight gain, headaches, increased blood pressure, acne, and depression.

Because it is a long-term implanted device, the IUD does not interrupt intercourse and it is cost-effective. It is a good kind of birth control for women who have had children and who are in long-term, one-on-one relationships in which the likelihood of STD infection is low. For these reasons, not many teens use IUDs; in general, it is not the ideal birth control for their lifestyles or time of life.

The Sponge

The Today Sponge, which is the contraceptive sponge that is allowed for sale in the United States currently, is a disk-shaped barrier that comes with a nylon loop for easy removal. Made from polyurethane foam, the sponge is infused with the spermicide nonoxynol-9. A woman wets the sponge before insertion, upside down, in the vagina. Although this birth control device does not protect either partner from STDs, it is said to be 89 percent to 91 percent effective, according to the Cleveland Clinic. It is less effective for women who have already had a child. An

The birth control patch, such as this one made by Ortho Evra, is a thin, beige, squarish patch that sticks to the skin. The patch is easy to use, but it can have similar side effects as the Pill, such as nausea and bleeding between periods.

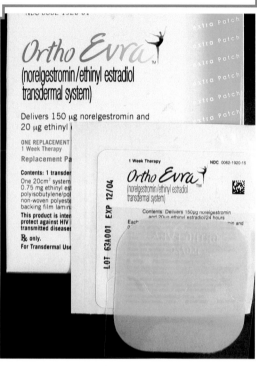

advantage to the sponge is that it can be inserted prior to sexual activity and remain in place for repeated activity over a twenty-four-hour period. The sponge, though, must be removed within thirty hours of insertion, but not until six hours have passed since the last ejaculation of sperm. You must pay careful attention to timing when using the sponge. Women who are allergic to nonoxynol-9 should not use this method of contraception.

The Birth Control Patch

The Patch, also called Ortho Evra after its brand name, is worn on the upper outer arm, upper torso (front and back, excluding the breasts), abdomen, or buttocks. The Patch contains the hormones progestin and estrogen, slowly releasing them through the skin and into the bloodstream. Women who use the Patch receive up to 60 percent more estrogen than they would on the Pill. A fresh Patch is applied once a week for three weeks, and then the fourth week in the cycle is skipped, allowing for menstruation to occur.

As noted by Planned Parenthood, the Patch, when used as directed, has been measured as 99 percent effective at preventing pregnancy, but it does not prevent STDs. Also, women weighing more than 198 pounds (90 kilograms) have a lower success rate with the Patch. Smokers should not use the Patch, as it can increase their risk of blood clots, strokes, and heart attacks.

The Vaginal Ring

The hormonal vaginal contraceptive ring, marketed under the name NuvaRing, works like the Patch. Rather than applied to the skin, however, is inserted into the vagina. The ring uses the same hormones as the Patch, although at much lower dosages. The ring is worn for three weeks and then removed for one week to allow for a period. After a week, a new ring is inserted.

Advantages of the ring include reduced menstrual cramps. The ring may also reduce the risk of ovarian cancer. The ring's disadvantages include potential menstrual cycle irregularities, especially during the first month, as well as weight gain, water retention, and breast tenderness. The FDA reports that the ring is about 98 percent to 99 percent effective at preventing pregnancy, but it does not prevent STDs. Your doctor will give you an examination before prescribing the ring.

Understanding Your Choices

You have many choices when it comes to birth control. Keep in mind, however, that abstinence is the only guaranteed way of preventing both pregnancy and sexually transmitted infections.

One of the best birth control choices is to use a method that protects against pregnancy and STDs, sometimes called doubling up. Many teens do this by using hormonal birth control (the Pill, Depo-Provera, or the Patch) and a male or female condom.

Talking with your partner about birth control is crucial. It is very important to use contraception each and every time you have sex. Couples who really care about each other want what is best for each other. This includes being free of disease or an unwanted pregnancy.

If you do have unprotected sex, take emergency contraception and get tested as soon as possible for STDs. Knowing the facts about birth control and your body will help you make good decisions today and in the future.

abnormality The peculiar characteristic of something that differs from what is normal or usual, typically in a way that is undesirable or worrying.

abstinence The practice of restraining oneself from having sex.

cervix The opening of the uterus.

clitoris The sensitive "bump" near the vagina, the stimulation of which contributes to a woman's orgasm.

contraceptive Birth control device.

ectopic In an unusual or wrong place; for example, an ectopic pregnancy is a pregnancy that is not in the uterus.

ejaculate To orgasm, or "come," and release semen.

estrogen A female hormone.

fallopian tubes Pair of tubes along which eggs travel from the ovaries to the uterus.

fertility The ability to reproduce and create offspring.

fertilize To create life; to begin pregnancy.

gynecologist A doctor who specializes in the female reproductive system.

hymen A layer of skin partially covering the opening of the vagina. Not all women are born with a hymen.

labia Lips of the vagina.

lubricate Make slippery or smooth; moisten.

masturbation Sexual self-stimulation.

menstrual cycle Also called menstruation, the monthly female fertility cycle (loss of blood and other matter from the uterus). Also called a "period."

orgasm The final stage of sexual stimulation that is marked by a female's vaginal contractions or the male's ejaculation.

ovaries Female organs that store and release a woman's eggs.

ovulation When an egg is released from an ovary into a fallopian tube.

penis Male sexual organ.

puberty Beginning of sexual, hormonal changes in the body.

pubic hair Hair covering or surrounding the genitals.

sperm Male fertilizing organism.

STDs Sexually transmitted diseases.

testicles Male sperm producers; contained in the scrotum and hanging outside the body below the lower abdomen and pelvis.

the Pill A contraceptive, taken orally; one of the most effective and popular forms of birth control.

unintended Accidental or unplanned.

uterus Womb, where a fetus grows and is nourished.

vagina Female sexual organ.

Advocates for Youth

Web site: http://www.advocatesforyouth.org/youth/
index.htm

Advocates for Youth is dedicated to creating programs and
working for policies that help young people make
informed and responsible decisions about their reproductive and sexual health.

American Social Health Organization

P.O. Box 13827

Research Triangle Park, NC 27709

(919) 361-8400

Web site: http://www.iwannaknow.org/index.html

The American Social Health Association operates the Web
site for Iwannaknow.org, which provides answers to
questions about teen sexual health and sexually transmitted diseases.

Association of Reproductive Health Professionals (ARHP)

2401 Pennsylvania Avenue NW, Suite 350

Washington, DC 20037

(202) 466-3825

Web site: http://www.arhp.org

The ARHP is a nonprofit membership association comprised of experts in reproductive health. Its members work to provide reproductive health services and education, conduct reproductive health research, and influence reproductive health policy.

Campaign for Our Children (CFOC)
One North Charles Street, Suite 1100
Baltimore, MD 21201
(410) 576-9015
Web site: http://www.cfoc.org/Home
CFOC addresses high teen birth rates through a comprehensive, hands-on program to educate children, parents, and the general public.

Centers for Disease Control and Prevention (CDC)
1600 Clifton Road
Atlanta, GA 30333
(800) 232-4636
Web site: http://www.cdc.gov
The CDC is the U.S. government's primary division for obtaining information on health and safety issues for the general public. Its Web site provides educational information about reproductive health and issues concerning teens.

ETR's Resource Center for Adolescent Pregnancy Prevention (ReCAPP)
Web site: http://www.etr.org/recapp

ETR is a private, nonprofit health-education promotion organization based in Santa Cruz, California. It offers state-of-the-art programs, professional training, and research in the area of adolescent pregnancy prevention.

National Campaign to Prevent Teen Pregnancy
1776 Massachusetts Avenue NW, Suite 200
Washington, DC 20036
(202) 478-8500
Web site: www.teenpregnancy.org
The National Campaign to Prevent Teen Pregnancy is a nonprofit initiative whose mission is to improve the well-being of children, youth, and families by reducing teen pregnancy.

National Women's Health Network
514 Tenth Street NW, Suite 400
Washington, DC 20005
(202) 347-1140
Web site: http://www.nwhn.org
The National Women's Health Network is committed to improving the health of all women by developing and promoting a critical analysis of health issues to alter policy and support consumer decision-making.

Options for Sexual Health
3550 East Hastings Street
Vancouver, BC V5K 2A7
Canada
(604) 731-4252

Web site: http://www.optionsforsexualhealth.org

Options for Sexual Health is a not-for-profit society meeting the reproductive and sexual health needs of British Columbians.

Planned Parenthood Federation of America

434 West Thirty-third Street

New York, NY 10001

(800) 230-7526

Web site: http://www.plannedparenthood.org

Planned Parenthood provides comprehensive reproductive and related health-care services in settings that preserve and protect the privacy and rights of each individual.

Sexual Health Access Alberta (SHAA)

1010, 1202 Centre Street SE

Calgary, AB T2G 5A5

Canada

(403) 283-8591

Web site: http://www.plannedparenthoodalta.com

Sexual Health Access Alberta provides education, advocacy, and leadership about sexual health issues impacting Albertans.

Sexuality Information and Education Council of the United States (SIECUS)

130 West Forty-second Street

New York, NY 10036

(212) 819-9770

Web site: http://www.siecus.org

SIECUS is a national voice for sexuality education, sexual health, and sexual rights. It advocates for the right of all people to accurate information, comprehensive education about sexuality, and sexual health services.

Teen Sex Infoline

(416) 961-3200

Web site: http://www.spiderbytes.ca

Maintained by young people, this infoline can be reached from 4 PM to 9 PM EST, Monday to Wednesday and 12 PM to 6 PM EST, Saturday and Sunday. Supported by Planned Parenthood of Toronto, the Web site is also staffed by youths who provide information on sexual health topics.

Teenwire.com

Web site: http://www.teenwire.com

Teenwire.com is an award-winning sexual health Web site for teens committed to giving young adults the facts about sex so that they can use this information to make their own responsible choices.

Web Sites

Due to the changing nature of Internet links, Rosen Publishing has developed an online list of Web sites related to the subject of this book. This site is updated regularly. Please use this link to access the list:

http://www.rosenlinks.com/faq/bctl

Bailey, Jacqui. *The Debate About Birth Control* (Ethical Debates). New York, NY: Rosen Publishing, 2010.

Blume, Judy. *Forever*. New York, NY: Simon Pulse, 2007.

Bronwen, Pardes. *Doing It Right: Making Smart, Safe, and Satisfying Choices About Sex*. New York, NY: Simon & Schuster, 2007.

Burchett, Katrina L. *Choices*. Jacksonville, FL: Kapri Books, 2007.

Feinstein, Stephen. *Sexuality and Teens. What You Should Know About Sex, Abstinence, Birth Control, Pregnancy, and STDs*. Berkeley Heights, NJ: Enslow Publishers, 2009.

Friedman, Lauri S. *Birth Control* (Introducing Issues with Opposing Viewpoints). Farmington Hills, MI: Greenhaven Press, 2009.

Frohnapfel-Krueger, Lisa. *Teen Pregnancy and Parenting* (Current Controversies). Farmington Hills, MI: Greenhaven Press, 2010.

Guillebaud, John, and Anne MacGregor. *The Pill and Other Forms of Hormonal Contraception* (The Facts). 7th ed. New York, NY: Oxford University Press, 2009.

Howard-Barr, Elissa, and Stacey M. Barrineau. *The Truth About Sexual Behavior and Unplanned Pregnancy*. New York, NY: Facts On File, 2009.

Hyde, Margaret, and Elizabeth Forsyth. *Safe Sex 101: An Overview for Teens*. New York, NY: Twenty-First Century Books, 2006.

Lawton, Sandra A., ed. *Sexual Health Information for Teens: Health Tips About Sexual Development, Reproduction, Contraception, and Sexually Transmitted Infections* (Teen Health Series). 2nd ed. Detroit, MI: Omnigraphics, Inc., 2008.

Libby, Roger W. *The Naked Truth About Sex: A Guide to Intelligent Sexual Choices for Teenagers and Twentysomethings*. Topanga, CA: Freedom Press, 2006.

Luadzers, Darcy. *Virgin Sex for Boys: A No-Regrets Guide for Safe and Healthy Sex*. Long Island City, NY: Hatherleigh Press, 2006.

Luadzers, Darcy. *Virgin Sex for Girls: A No-Regrets Guide for Safe and Healthy Sex*. Long Island City, NY: Hatherleigh Press, 2006.

MacKay, Jennifer. *Teen Pregnancy* (Hot Topics). Farmington Hills, MI: Lucent Books, 2011.

Magill, Elizabeth, ed. *Sexual Health Information for Teens: Health Tips About Sexual Development, Reproduction, Contraception, and Sexually Transmitted Infections* (Teen Health Series). 3rd ed. Detroit, MI: Omnigraphics, Inc., 2011.

Merino, Noel. *Birth Control* (Issues on Trial). Farmington Hills, MI: Greenhaven Press, 2010.

Rosenthal, Beth. *Birth Control* (Opposing Viewpoints). Farmington Hills, MI: Greenhaven Press, 2008.

Saulmon, Greg. *Genital Herpes* (The Library of Sexual Health). New York, NY: Rosen Publishing, 2007.

Stanley, Cleo, and Carolyn Simpson. *I'm Pregnant. Now What?* (Teen Life 411). New York, NY: Rosen Publishing, 2012.

St. Stephen's Community House. *The Little Black Book for Girlz: A Book on Healthy Sexuality.* Toronto, ON: Annick Press, 2006.

Waters, Sophie. *Seeing the Gynecologist* (Girls' Health). New York, NY: Rosen Publishing, 2008.

West, Krista. *Urinary Tract Infections* (The Library of Sexual Health). New York, NY: Rosen Publishing, 2007.

Zonderman, Jon, and Laurel Shader. *Birth Control Pills.* (Drugs: The Straight Facts). New York, NY: Chelsea House Publishers, 2006.

About the Authors

Beverly Vincent is a writer who lives in Ionia County, Michigan.

Robert Greenberger has written several nonfiction books for young adults, including works on the natural sciences, careers, and technology. He lives in Connecticut.

Photo Credits

Cover Peter Cade/Iconica/Getty Images; pp. 5, 25 Stockbyte/ Stockbyte/Thinkstock; p. 7 © www.istockphoto.com/Sean Locke; pp. 11, 13 Nucleus Medical Art, Inc./Getty Images; p. 14 Science Picture Co/Science Faction/Getty Images; p. 19 Spencer Grant/ Photo Researchers; p. 20 Shutterstock; p. 30 A. Wilson/ Custom Medical Stock Photo; p. 33 FemCap Inc and Alfred Shihata, MD; p. 37 © AP Images; p. 40 Aaron Haupt/Photo Researchers; p. 42 AJPhoto/Photo Researchers; p. 45 Dr. P. Marazzi/Photo Researchers; p. 47 Science Photo Library/Getty Images; p. 49 Custom Medical Stock Photo.

Designer: Nicole Russo; Photo Researcher: Marty Levick